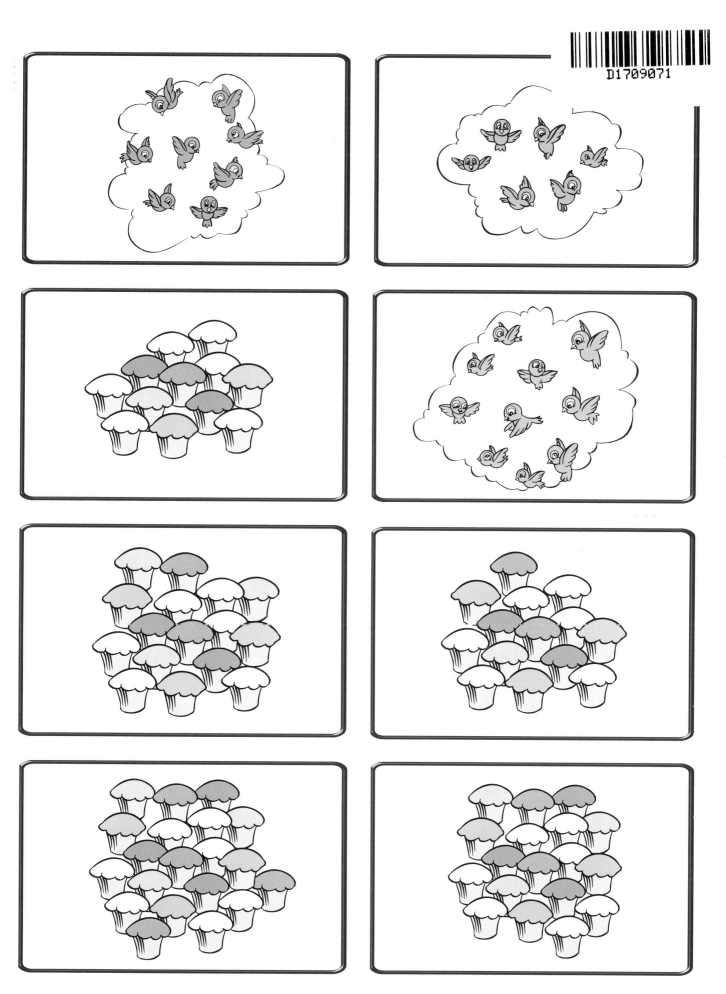

How many items are on each card?

six

eight

ten

twelve

fourteen

sixteen

eighteen

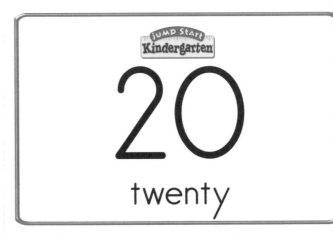

twenty

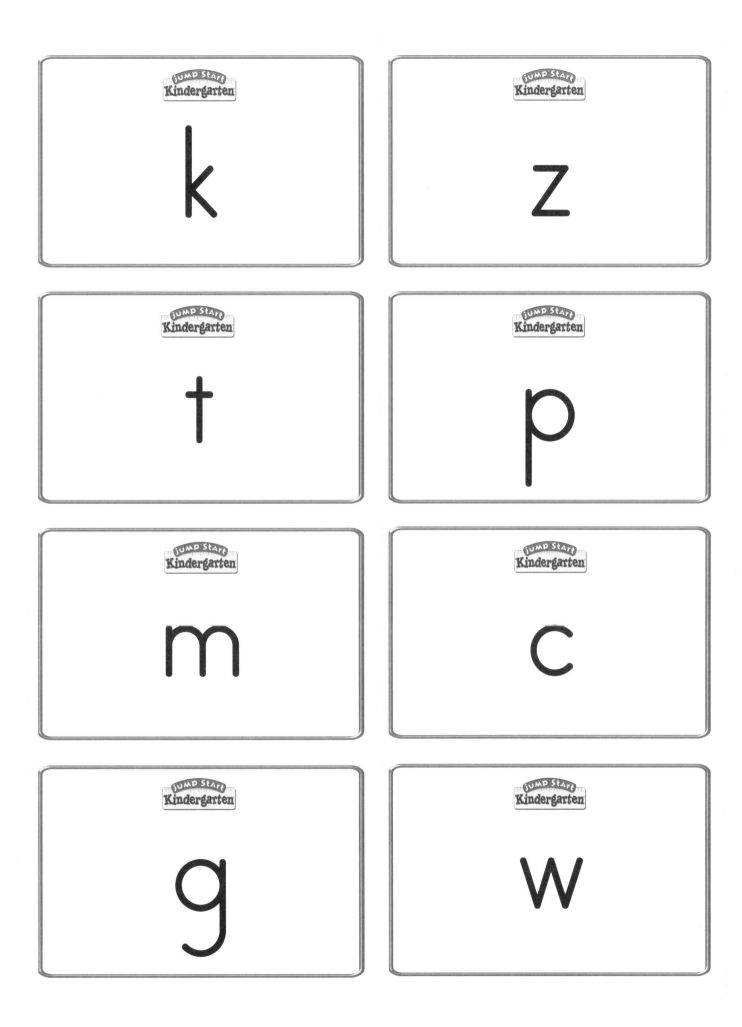

__ebra

__angaroo

__ig

__iger

__at

__onkey

__alrus

__oat

What is the first letter in each word?

Lowercase Letters

Hi, there! It's your pal, Hopsalot! Are you ready for some ABC fun in the schoolhouse? First, grab a pencil and some crayons. But come back fast—I can't wait to hop inside!

See these carrots? Every time you learn something new, you get a carrot sticker to put in your picnic basket. When you finish a whole section, you'll get a big flag sticker to decorate your Certificate of Completion at the end of the book.

Look for this picture of me! When you see it, it means I'm there to give you a little help. Just look for **Hopsalot's Hints**.

Ready?
Let's hop
to it!

Hopsalot's Hints

Tracing is great practice! Just follow the numbers as you trace each line.

Jumping gerbils! School sure looks fun! Let's start at the writing center. **Trace and write each letter on the lines.**

Can you find something in this picture that starts with the sound of "a," as in alligator?

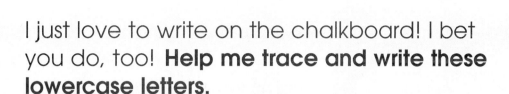

I just love to write on the chalkboard! I bet you do, too! **Help me trace and write these lowercase letters.**

c c

d d

e e

Awesome! Put your carrot sticker in your picnic basket and let's keep going.

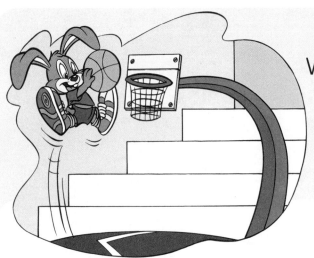

Whew! I am tired from playing hoops! **Can you help me trace and write these lowercase letters?**

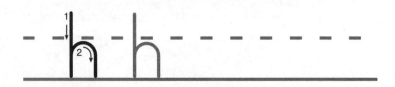

Can you find something on this page that begins with the sound of "h," as in hippo?

Guess what? The gym teacher is a kangaroo! **Can you trace and write these letters while we hop?**

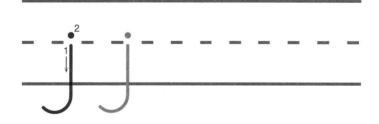

You did a hopping good job! Now say something that begins with the sound of "k," as in kite.

All that hopping makes me hungry! Good thing it's time for lunch. **While I get a tray, can you trace and write each letter below?**

I love milk! It starts with the sound of "m." Can you find something in this lunchroom that begins with the sound of "l"?

Yummy! I am having pizza for lunch!

While I eat, you can trace and write the lowercase letters below.

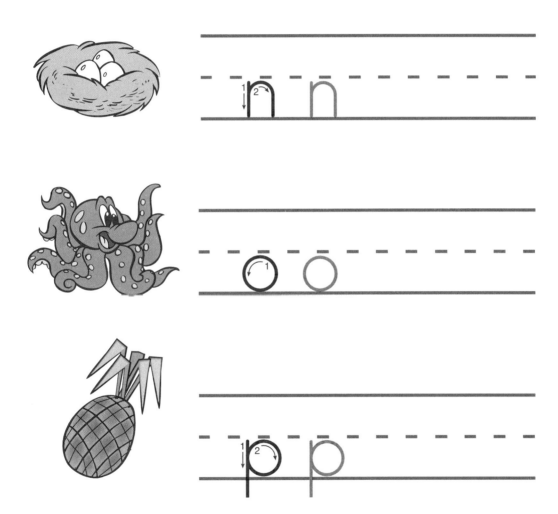

Neat-o! Perfect printing! Put a carrot sticker in your picnic basket.

Lowercase Letters   7

Here we are in the library, my favorite place!
While I read my book, you can trace and write the letters below.

Now find something else on this page that begins with the sound of "r," as in rose. Hint: It has long ears and it likes to hop!

My friend Bebop digs the music room! Gracie thinks it's fun, too! **While we make music and dance, trace and write the letters below.**

Can you think of something else that starts with the letter s? How about the letter t? The letter u?

Stupendous! Toe-tapping, too! Put your carrot sticker in the picnic basket.

Wow! My school has everything—even a garden!
While I take a juicy watermelon break, can you
trace and write the letters below?

Find two things
on this page
that start with
the sound
of "w," as in
wagon.

Look at me! I am playing my favorite game at recess—xyz hopscotch! You can play, too!

First, trace and write the letters x, y, and z.

Can you think of something else that starts with y? What about z?

Excellent! Put the JumpStart school flag on your Certificate of Completion! Then jump ahead.

Hopsalot's Hints

This **a** is **lowercase**. This **A** is **uppercase**. Each letter of the alphabet can be written in both lowercase and uppercase letters.

I bet you love books as much as I do! **Draw a line from each lowercase book to the matching uppercase book.**

a b c

D E F

d e f

J K L

g h i

A B C

j k l

G H I

Can you circle the uppercase and lowercase letter that begins my name?

Flash is in a hurry to get to class! **Can you help him? Draw lines to match the uppercase letters to the same letters in lowercase.**

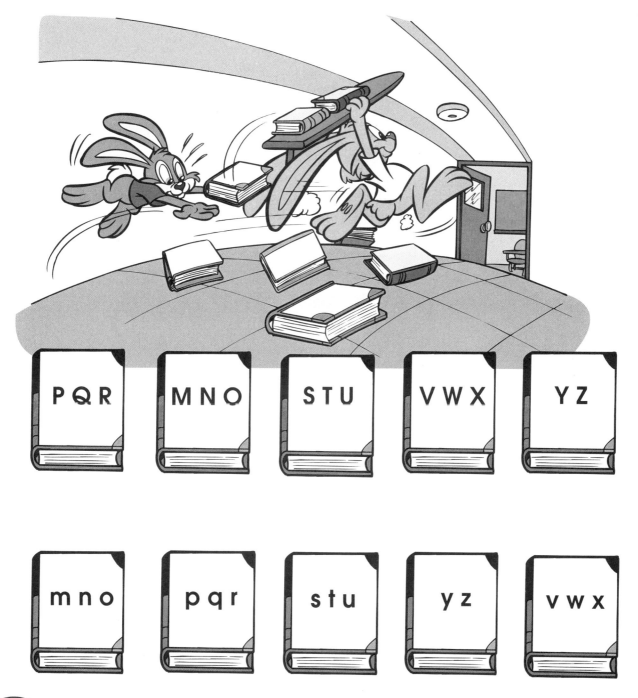

P Q R   M N O   S T U   V W X   Y Z

m n o   p q r   s t u   y z   v w x

Great job! Put your carrot sticker in your basket and jump ahead to the next level.

Hopsalot's Hints

You can sing the **ABC** song to help you remember the order of the letters.

Bebop is helping me learn to juggle clubs. Too bad we keep dropping them! Help us put the clubs in ABC order. **On the lines below, write the missing letters. Look at the clubs to the left.**

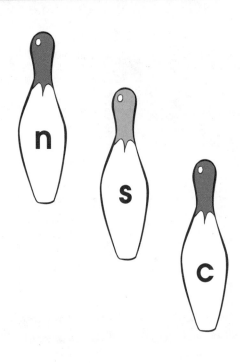

a b ☐ d

t m ☐ o p

☐ t u v

w x y z

Stupendous! Now circle the club that has the first letter in the word carrot.

It's so much fun to play ABC games on the computer! Can you help me with this one? **Write the missing letters in ABC order on the screens.**

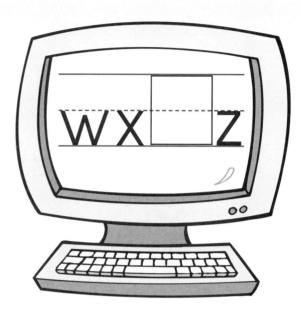

w x ☐ z

☐ i j k

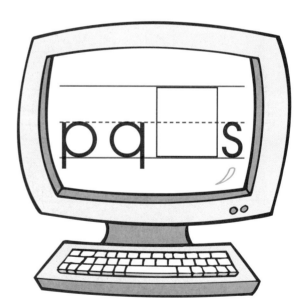

p q ☐ s

It's cleanup time! Help me put the blocks back on the shelves. **Write the missing letters on the blocks in ABC order.**

a b ___ d

e ___ g ___

i j ___ ___

c f h l k

Are any of these letters in your name? Circle each one that is.

My friends Gracie and Einstein are decorating the classroom for a party. Some of the balloons are missing letters. **Write the letters in ABC order on the balloons. Einstein's balloons tell you which letters are missng.**

I love to cook in school! This is my prize-winning alphabet chili! **Write the letters in ABC order on the lines next to each bowl. Remember: Some should be uppercase, and some should be lower!**

NLKM

oqpr

acb

SUT

FEGD

vxw

hji

ZY

How many alphabet letters in the bowls are lowercase? _____

How many are uppercase? _____

Hopsalot's Hints

The uppercase letters C, O, S, and W look a little bit like their lowercase letters. Other uppercase letters, like A, B, E, and G, look different from their lowercase letters.

Can you help me wash these dishes? **Put the scrambled letters in ABC order. Write them on the lines next to the soap bubbles.**

mln

_____

OQP

_____

CDAB

_____

fge

_____

JHIK

_____

You really cleaned up! Put a carrot sticker in your basket and jump ahead to see what you've learned.

ABC Order 19

Can you help me with my giant treat? **Connect the dots from lowercase a to lowercase z. Then connect the dots from uppercase A to uppercase Z. Boy, this is heavy!**

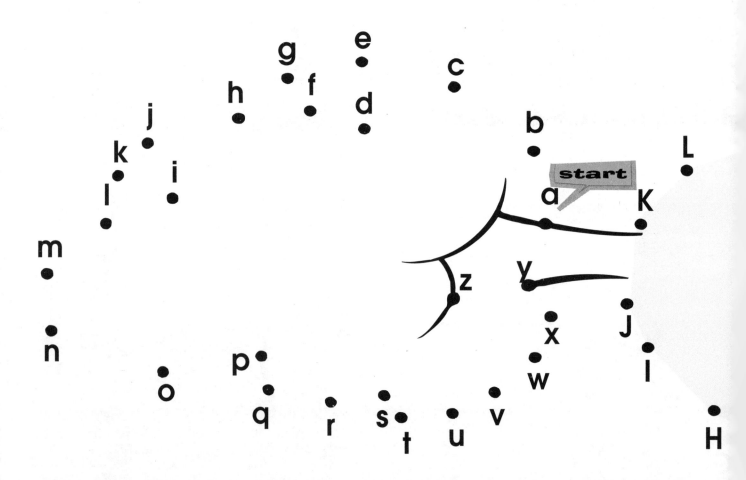

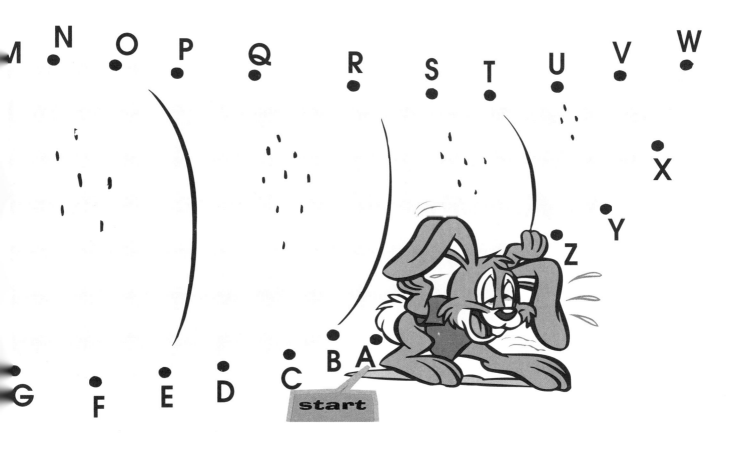

M N O P Q R S T U V W X Y Z G F E D C B A start

Super-duper! Put your letter flag on your Certificate of Completion. Then jump ahead for more letter fun.

Review 21

Hopsalot's Hints

Say each picture word below aloud. Listen carefully for the first sound.

 and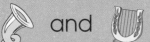

Both begin with the sound of **h**.

It's time for music with Bebop! **Help me draw lines to match each musical instrument with something that begins with the same sound.**

Can you name another instrument and something else that begins with the same sound?

Look at all the things in my classroom! **Can you draw lines between the objects that begin with the same sound?**

Terrific! Put a carrot sticker in your basket and jump ahead to the next level.

Letter Sounds **23**

Presto! Help me change these letters into dress-up clothes! **Draw a line from each letter to the picture with the same beginning sound.**

b

t

h

w

p

I really love to paint! Look at all of my pictures. **Draw a line from each picture to the letter that names the beginning sound.**

f

r

v

n

d

m

On a separate piece of paper, draw a picture of something else that starts with the sound of "m" or "d."

Matching letters and sounds is hard work! Bebop and I are taking a picnic break. **Draw lines to help us match these picture names with their beginning letter sounds.**

j l s a g c

Can you name another food with the same beginning sound as corn? Hint: It's my favorite!

I'm bouncing my ball and Flash is hopping on his pogo stick. **Match these objects to the letters with the same beginning sound.**

z   k   e   y   g   q

Great job! Put a carrot sticker in your basket and jump ahead to the next level.

Letter Sounds   27

Level 2

Hopsalot's Hints

Say each picture word below aloud. Listen for the first sound.

and both begin with the sound of **b**.

Let's play tic-tac-toe!
Say each picture name. Then write the letter with the sound you hear at the beginning of each name.

Now find the row with pictures that have the same first sound. Draw a line through them to win the game!

Let's play again! **Write the first letter in each picture name.**

Now find three in a row that have the same first sound. Draw a line through that row. You win again!

Tic-Tac-Terrific! Put a carrot sticker in your basket and jump ahead.

Letter Sounds (29)

Now it's time to go home. Help me get back to the carrot patch! **Write the first letter for each picture name on the path. Use lowercase letters.**

Now draw a line connecting the letters in ABC order from the JumpStart School to the carrot patch.

Go to the head of the class! Put your ABC flag sticker on your Certificate of Completion. Hooray!

Review (31)

Answer Key

PAGE 2 write a,b; find a/apple

PAGE 3 write c, d, e

PAGE 4 write f, g, h; find h/hoop; Hopsalot

PAGE 5 write i, j, k; answers will vary

PAGE 6 write l, m; find l/lion

PAGE 7 write n, o, p

PAGE 8 write q, r; find r/rabbit

PAGE 9 write s, t, u; answers will vary

PAGE 10 write v, w; find w/web,worm, wheelbarrow, watermelon

PAGE 11 write x, y, z; answers will vary

PAGE 12 abc/ABC; def/DEF; ghi/GHI; jkl/JKL; H, h

PAGE 13 PQR/pqr; MNO/mno; STU/stu; VWX/vwx; YZ/yz

PAGE 14 c, n, s; circle the club with the c on it

PAGE 15 y, h, r

PAGE 16 c, f, h, k, l; circle letters in your name

PAGE 17 s, u, w, z

PAGE 18 KLMN; opqr; abc; STU; DEFG; vwx; hij; YZ; 13; 13

PAGE 19 lmn, OPQ , ABCD, efg, HIJK

PAGES 20–21 dot-to-dot: giant carrot with leafy top

PAGE 22 piano/penguin; guitar/goat; triangle/truck; drum/dress; violin/vase

PAGE 23 book/basketball; doll/duck; ink/igloo; elephant/envelope

PAGE 24 b/boots; t/tie; h/hat; w/wig; p/pants

PAGE 25 f/fish; r/rabbit; v/vase; n/nest; d/dog, m/moon

PAGE 26 j/jelly; l/lettuce; s/sandwich; a/apple; g/grapes; c/corn; carrot

PAGE 27 z/zipper; k/kite; e/egg; y/yarn; g/goat; q/quarter

PAGE 28 cat, bee, hat, sun, soap, saw; sock, duck, bone; draw a line through sun, soap, saw

PAGE 29 zebra, apple, table, bed, tire, carrot; pig, pan, pencil; draw a line through pig, pan, pencil

PAGES 30–31 a/apple, b/bird, c/carrot, d/duck, e/egg, f/fan, g/goat, h/house, i/igloo, j/jumprope, k/kite, l/lamp, m/moon, n/nut, o/owl, p/piano, q/quarter, r/rabbit, s/sun, t/turtle, u/umbrella, v/violin, w/wig, x/xray, y/yo-yo, z/zebra

Reading Readiness

Hi there! It's your pal, Hopsalot! Are you ready for some reading fun? I sure hope so. Grab a pencil and some crayons, and let's hop along!

See these carrots? Every time you learn something new, you get one of these stickers to put in your picnic basket. When you finish a whole section, you'll get a big flag sticker to decorate your Certificate of Completion at the end of the book.

Here I am with my carrot. When you see this picture of me, it means I'm there to give you a little help. Just look for **Hopsalot's Hints**.

Ready? Let's hop to it!

This street sure is busy! Help me drive down the road. **Say the name of each vehicle, then draw a line to the picture name with the same beginning sound.**

We're ready for our first field trip! Help me fill up at the gas station. **Say the picture name on each gas pump. Then draw a line to match up the pumps with the same beginning sound.**

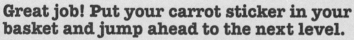
Great job! Put your carrot sticker in your basket and jump ahead to the next level.

Beginning Sounds **35**

Our first stop is the apple orchard! Look at this juicy red apple! What else do we have here? **Name everything on the table. Then draw a line to the letter that stands for the beginning sound.**

a   s   d   f   y   j

Apple begins with the "a" sound. The letter a makes the "a" sound. Can you find and circle something else in the picture that begins with the letter a?

Uh-oh! It's raining! Quick! Help me stay dry.
Say each picture name and listen for the beginning sound. Then draw a line to the umbrella with the matching letter.

b   n   h   r   l

What came out after the rain? ——
Write the beginning letter to ---------
complete the word. ____ un

Our next stop is the zoo! Let's feed the animals. **Say the name of each animal, then draw a line from each bowl to the animal with the same beginning sound.**

Circle the hungry animal.
What letter does his name start with?

_____

- - - - - - - - - - - - - - - -

_____

What big animals do you see at the zoo?
**Say the name of each animal. Then write the letter that stands for the beginning sound.
Choose from these sounds:**

w z t k

_____

_____ angaroo

_____

_____ alrus

_____

_____ ebra

_____

_____ iger

Zoo-pendous! Put your carrot sticker in your basket and jump ahead to the next level!

Hopsalot's Hints

Say the picture name aloud. Listen for the beginning sound. **P-eas**. Peas begins with the "**p**" sound.

Yum! Yum! Visiting the vegetable farm is my favorite school trip! **Write the first letter of each picture name on the lines.**

_____ arrots

_____ omatoes

_____ ucumbers

_____ adishes

_____ ettuce

_____ eans

On to the beach! Flash is trying to teach me how to sail! **Be a good sailor and write the first letter to complete each word before we land in the water!**

___ eal

___ alrus

___ olphin

___ ire

___ ish

Sea-pendous sailing job! Put your carrot sticker in your basket and jump ahead!

Up, up and away! Let's play a game. **Open the book so it lays flat. Toss a coin onto the game board and see what letter it lands on. Then name something that begins with the same sound and letter. Name as many things as you can for each letter.**

Two can play by taking turns!

Terrific tossing! Put your big flag sticker on the Certificate of Completion. Then jump ahead!

Review 43

Hopsalot's Hints

The **ending sound** is the last sound you hear in a word. Dog ends with the "**g**" sound.

Here we are at the circus! **Say the names of everything in the rings. Can you find the words that have the same ending sound? Draw lines to match them.**

rug

mitt

man

dog

clown

hat

I think I'll stop the bus and rest for a bit. **While I stretch my legs, you can draw lines to match the picture names with the same ending sounds.**

bird

owl

squirrel

cloud

wagon

van

Stupendous work! Put your carrot sticker in your basket and jump ahead to the next level!

Ending Sounds (45)

Look! Yummy chocolates from Grandma! **Say each picture name. Listen for the ending sound, then write l, n, or t on the line.**

spoo ___

came ___

hear ___

ca ___

bel ___

balloo ___

Grandma's chocolates were delicious! I think I'll stop the bus at the Sweet Shop and get a present for her! **Write m, l, or n to finish each word.**

Sweet Shop

wor ____

gu ____

bal ____

bel ____

trai ____

Let's go back to the sea! **While Flash teaches me how to ride his surfboard, write d, t, g, or k to complete each word.**

fla _____

rowboa _____

surfboar _____

raf _____

shar _____

Good surfing! Now circle the two words that end in the same sound.

What a fun day at the beach! Now it's time to dry off. **Before we go, write the letter that stands for the ending sound in each word. Write d, l, b, or n on the lines.**

cra _____

towe _____

seawee _____

fa _____

shove _____

su _____

Hopsalot's Hints

Rhyming words have the same middle and ending sounds, but different beginning sounds. **Cap** and **map** are rhyming words.

I am lost for sure! Luckily, Romulus's ranch is nearby. **While I ask Romulus for directions, write n or g to finish each word. Which words rhyme?**

ju _____   mu _____

he _____   pe _____

cor _____   hor _____

Driving the bus is hard work! Let's take a look at a book in the brook! **Each sentence below has two rhyming words. Can you write g, t, or x at the end of each word?**

A **fro** ___ sits on a **lo** ___ .

A **fo** ___ sleeps on a **bo** ___ .

The **an** ___ crawls on the **plan** ___ .

Look at this beautiful butterfly! Help us color it in.
Read the word in each space. Color the spaces that rhyme with:

sail = green

coat = blue

rock = yellow

stop = red

plug = brown

well = orange

mat = purple

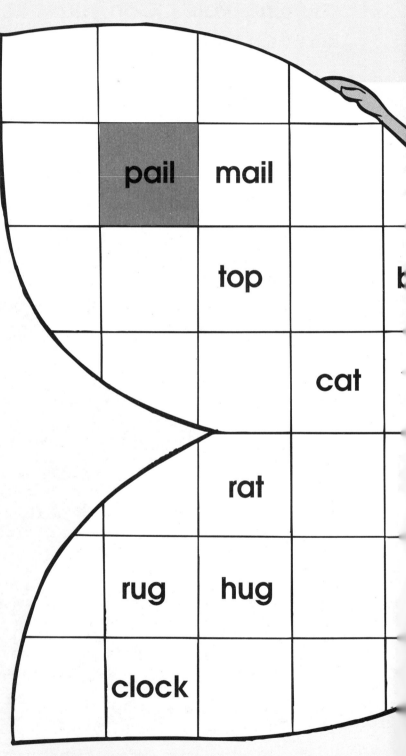

pail   mail

top   b

cat

rat

rug   hug

clock

Color in the blank spaces any color you like!

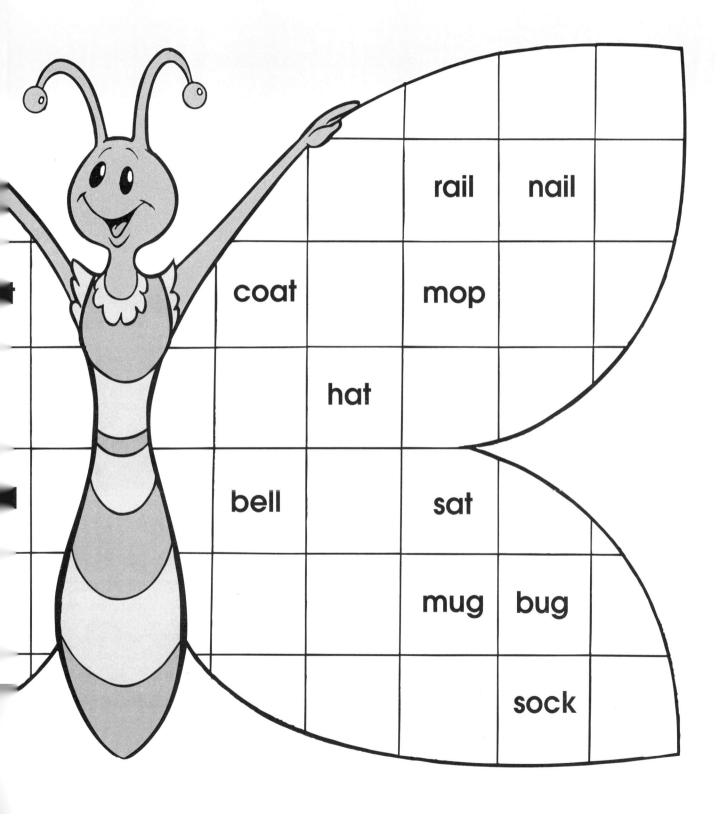

rail | nail

coat | mop

hat

bell | sat

mug | bug

sock

upendous rhyming! Put your big flag sticker on your
rtificate of Completion and jump ahead.

Review 53

Hopsalot's Hints

Try listening for the middle sound. In the word "**log**" the first sound you hear is "**l**." The middle sound is "**o**." The ending sound is "**g**."

l-**o**-g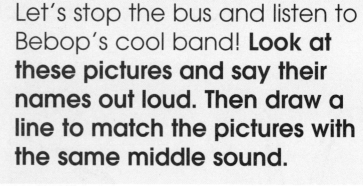

Let's stop the bus and listen to Bebop's cool band! **Look at these pictures and say their names out loud. Then draw a line to match the pictures with the same middle sound.**

Oh, no! A flat tire! **While I change it, can you say the name of each picture out loud? Draw a line to match the pictures with the same middle sound.**

Flat-abulous! Put your carrot sticker in your basket and jump ahead to the next level!

Middle Sounds **55**

I need help! Let's get the tire fixed at the gas station. Then we can be on our way! **While we wait, draw lines between the pictures with the same middle sound. Each picture has two matches.**

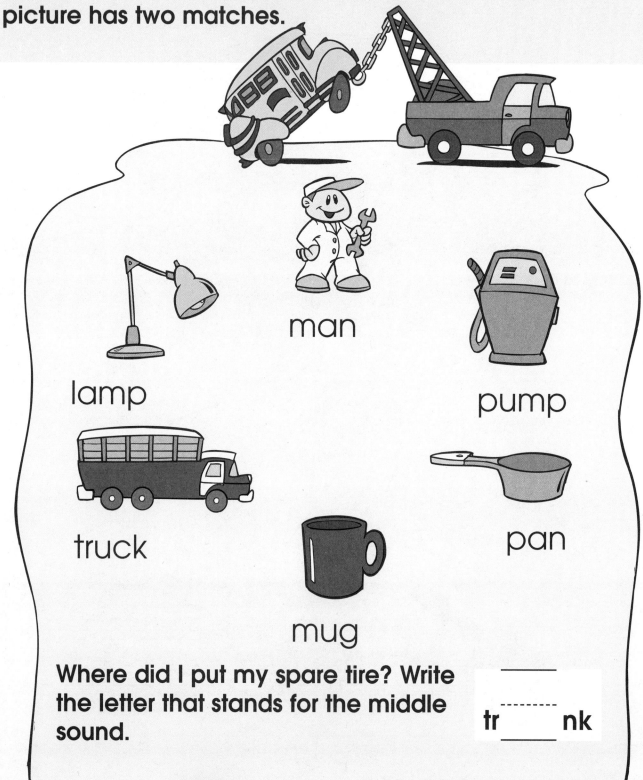

man

lamp

pump

truck

pan

mug

Where did I put my spare tire? Write the letter that stands for the middle sound.

tr __ nk

The bus is fixed and the gas tank is full! Now it's time to fill up the driver! **While I eat, write the letter that stands for the middle sound in each word. Write a, i, or o.**

| a | | | | | |

Good work! Now, can you change the middle sound in 🪣 to make a word on the page?

Hint: I am wearing one!

c ___ p

It's a pop-fly ball! Catch it, Gracie! **While we play ball, match the letter on each mitt to the picture name with the same middle sound.**

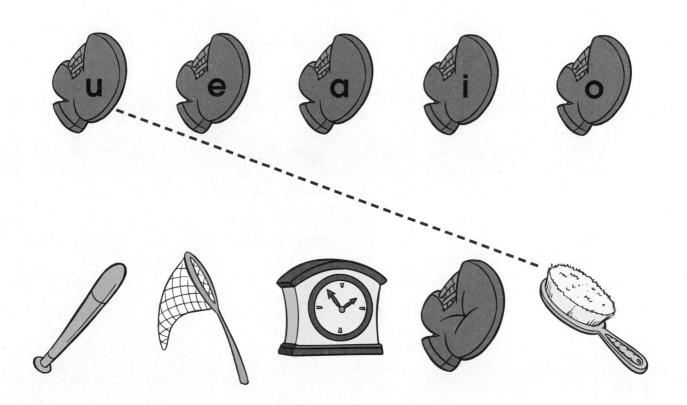

You batted in those middle sounds! Good job! What happened to that ball? Write a to find out.

____

It is in my   h ____ nd !

Flash and I love to watch the jets at the airport!
Before the next jet takes off, match each picture on the ramp to the letter that stands for the middle sound.

a	e	i	o	u

Up, up, and away! Put your carrot sticker in your basket and jump ahead to the next level!

Middle Sounds　59

Hopsalot's Hints

The letter **a** stands for the middle sound in **hat**.
The letter **i** stands for the middle sound in **hit**.
The letter **o** stands for the middle sound in **hot**.

hat

hit

hot

One of Flash's favorite field trips is to the playground.
Write the letter that stands for the middle sound in all the things Flash and I are doing. Write a, u, i, or o.

h ___ ng

r ___ n

h ___ p

sl ___ p

After all those trips, I am beat!
I think I will take a nap in
the school bus. **While I
sleep, write the missing
letter in each word.
Use a, e, i, o, or u.**

The **sh** _i_ **p** looks like a **sh** _o_ **p** .

The **b** ___ **g** is on the **r** ___ **g** .

The **d** ___ **g** can **d** ___ **g** .

The **b** ___ **t** **b** ___ **t** it .

You will need a die and a coin to mark your spot. Two people can play. **Each player should have a different color crayon. Roll the die and move that many spaces on the board. Then read the word and find the matching picture on the board.**

cat

bag

hat

man

mat

Start

sun

hog

hut

pod

mug

hat

core

truck

log

bug

bug

grass

crib

mat

sun

pod

crib

log

Mark an X in your color on that picture. Then mark an X on any other picture with the same middle sound. After you have both reached FINISH, the player with the most X's wins.

pen

bed

plane

hen

grass

lips

bib

box

pen

man

bag

fox

cat

cup

lips

bib

bed

plane

hog

hit

hut

hen

Finish

box

fox

apple

hit

upendous playing! Put your big flag sticker on e Certificate of Completion. You are flying high!

Review 63

Answer Key

PAGE 34   car/cookie; van/vest; bike/balloon; motorcycle/moon; wagon/web

PAGE 35   kite/key; donut/dog; hammer/helicopter; ring/robot

PAGE 36   doll/d; fork/f; sandwich/s; jelly/j; yo-yo/y; ants

PAGE 37   n/nest; r/raincoat; b/boots; h/hat; l/leaf; sun

PAGE 38   g/goat; c/cat; m/monkey; r/rabbit; p/pig; g

PAGE 39   kangaroo/k; walrus/w; zebra/z; tiger/t

PAGE 40   t/tomatoes; c/carrots; c/cucumbers; r/radishes; l/lettuce; b/beans

PAGE 41   s/seal; w/walrus; d/dolphin; t/tire; f/fish

PAGES 42–43 Answers will vary.

PAGE 44   mitt/hat; rug/dog; man/clown

PAGE 45   owl/squirrel; cloud/bird; van/wagon

PAGE 46   n/spoon; l/camel; t/heart; t/cat; l/bell; n/balloon

PAGE 47   m/worm; l/ball; m/gum; n/train; l/bell

PAGE 48   g/flag; t/rowboat; d/surfboard; t/raft; k/shark; circle rowboat/raft

PAGE 49   b/crab; l/towel; d/seaweed; n/fan; l/shovel; n/sun

PAGE 50   g/jug; g/mug; n/hen; n/pen; n/corn; n/horn

PAGE 51   g/frog; g/log; x/fox; x/box; t/ant; t/plant

PAGES 52–53 color green: pail, mail, rail, nail; color blue: boat, coat; color yellow: clock, sock; color red: top, mop; color brown: rug, hug, mug, bug; color orange: shell, bell; color purple: cat, hat, rat, sat

PAGE 54   cat/hat; frog/log; sled/bed

PAGE 55   mop/pot; fish/ship; bug/mug

PAGE 56   a/man, lamp, pan; u/pump, truck, mug; trunk

PAGE 57   a/lamp, stamp; i/milk, fish; o/mop, fox; cap

PAGE 58   u/brush; e/net; a/bat; i/mitt; o/clock; hand

PAGE 59   cat/a; box/o; rug/u; dress/e; bricks/i

PAGE 60   a/hang; u/run; o/hop; i/slip

PAGE 61   l/ship; u/rug; o/shop; u/bug; o/dog; i/dig; a/bat; i/bit

PAGES 62–63 Answers will vary.

Math Readiness

Hi! It's your pal Hopsalot, and look what we just got! It's an invitation to Guthry the Giant's birthday party in Cloud Town! Cloud Town is way up there in the sky. So, get ready. We have a whole new world to explore!

See these carrots? Every time you finish learning something new, you get one of these stickers to put in your picnic basket. When you finish each section, you get a big flag sticker to put on your Certificate of Completion.

Take a look at this picture of me. When you see this picture, it means I'm there to share hints to help you. Just look for **Hopsalot's Hints**.

Are you ready? Great! Grab a leaf and let's start to climb!

Hopsalot's Hints

When you count, it helps to **touch** each thing as you say the number.

The magic bean I planted grew into a giant beanstalk! **Count the magic beans on each leaf. Then trace the number.**

Climbing magic beanstalks is hard work! I think I will rest a while and watch the clouds. **Count the birds and trace the numbers. Then color in the clouds.**

Wonderful work! Put your carrot sticker in your basket and jump ahead to the next level!

Counting 67

The sky is a very busy place in Cloud Town! Look at all the little clouds! **Connect the dots next to the clouds from 1 to 20 to see what else is in the sky.**

Baker Jake is making cupcakes for the party! While I clean the bowl, you can count the cupcakes on the plates below. **Write the numbers on the lines.**

| 1 | 2 | 3 | 4 | 5 | 6 | 7 | 8 | 9 | 10 | 11 | 12 | 13 | 14 | 15 | 16 | 17 | 18 | 19 | 20 |

_____
- - - - - - - - - - - - - - -
_____

_____
- - - - - - - - - - - - - - -
_____

_____
- - - - - - - - - - - - - - -
_____

_____
- - - - - - - - - - - - - - -
_____

_____
- - - - - - - - - - - - - - -
_____

How many cupcakes have pink frosting?

_____
- - - - - - - - - - - - - - -
_____

Too-Loose the Tailor is making a new shirt for Guthry. Here are some more shirts! **Count the buttons on each one. Then write the number.**

3

Can you count how many buttons there are altogether?

Breezy the cat has been blowing up balloons all morning. But where did they go? Can you help me find them? **Circle each balloon. Count them out loud as you go. Can you find all 20?**

Good job! Put your carrot sticker in your basket and jump ahead to the next level!

Counting 71

Hopsalot's Hints

When you are counting many things, **cross out** each thing you count. That way you can be sure you don't count the same thing twice.

Now Baker Jake is baking giant cookies for Guthry's party! **Count the raisins on the cookies below. Write the numbers on the lines.**

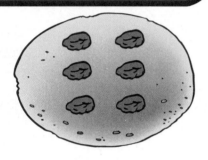

_____

- - - - - - - - - - - - - - - -

_____

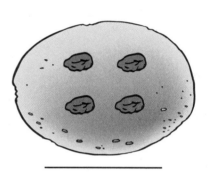

_____

- - - - - - - - - - - - - - - -

_____

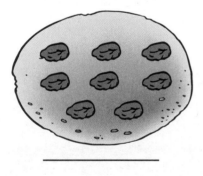

_____

- - - - - - - - - - - - - - - -

_____

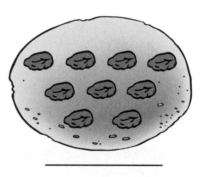

_____

- - - - - - - - - - - - - - - -

_____

How many raisins did Baker Jake use on the cookies altogether? Count them all.

_____

- - - - - - - - - - - - - - - -

_____

I am helping Baker Jake put the raisins on the cookies! Can you help, too? **Draw the number of raisins shown on the bag on each cookie.**

Now count up all of the raisins you've drawn. How many are there in all?

Stupendous! Put your carrot sticker in your basket and jump ahead!

Someone from Cloud Town is hidden here.
Connect the dots from 1 to 30 to see who is hiding.
Then color the picture.

Hopsalot's Hints

When you have many things to count, **skip-counting by tens** will make the job go faster. Skip-count to **50** by tens:
10, 20, 30, 40, 50

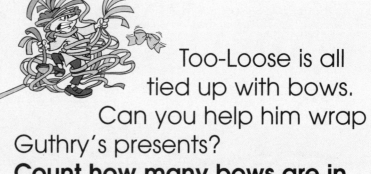

Too-Loose is all tied up with bows. Can you help him wrap Guthry's presents? **Count how many bows are in each group, and write the number on the line.**

_____

- - - - - - - - - - - - - - - - -

_____

_____

- - - - - - - - - - - - - - - - -

_____

_____

- - - - - - - - - - - - - - - - -

_____

_____

- - - - - - - - - - - - - - - - -

_____

You are the counting champ! Now skip-count by tens to see how many bows there are altogether.

_____

- - - - - - - - - - - - - - - - -

_____

It is raining gumdrops in Cloud Town!
Count each group of gumdrops. Write how many there are on the line.

_____

_____

_____

_____

Sweetly done! Now skip-count by tens to see how many gumdrops there are altogether.

_____

_____

_____

Super! Put your carrot sticker in your basket and jump ahead to the next level!

Counting by Groups (77)

I've got to pick up some packages at the post office right away. Good thing I can hop 10 steps at a time! **Count the steps out loud. Then color in the steps I'll hop on if I hop 10 steps at a time.**

POST OFFICE

How many steps did I hop on to reach the post office?

_____

- - - - - - - - - - - - - - -

_____

The children in Cloud Town are helping Baker Jake carry some giant cupcakes. **How many children are helping altogether? Write the numbers on the cupcakes.**

How many
children in all?
Count by tens.

Count the fingers on one hand. When you **skip-count by fives**, you are counting a handful!

**5, 10, 15, 20, 25
All end in 0 or 5.**

Hopsalot and Farmer Hank need your help with this wrapping paper. **Count the rectangles of each color and write the number at the bottom.**

5 _____ _____ _____ _____

How many rectangles are there altogether on the wrapping paper? Skip-count by fives. _____

Dash is helping us decorate for the party. Help her skip-count the groups of balloons by fives.
Write the number on the line.

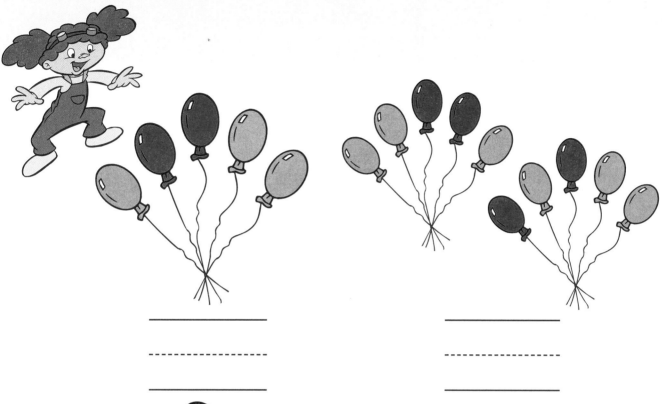

_____

_____

_____

_____

How many balloons are there altogether?

_____

_____

_____

_____

Good job! Put your carrot sticker in your basket and jump ahead to the next level!

Counting by Groups (81)

Hopsalot's Hints

Counting by ones is slow. **Skip-counting by twos** is faster. Say these numbers:

1 2 3 4 5 6 7 8 9 10

Now skip every other number:

2 4 6 8 10

See the difference?

Dash found a box of giant candles for Guthry's cake. **Can you skip-count them by twos and write how many there are?**

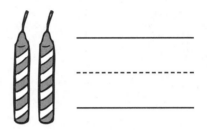

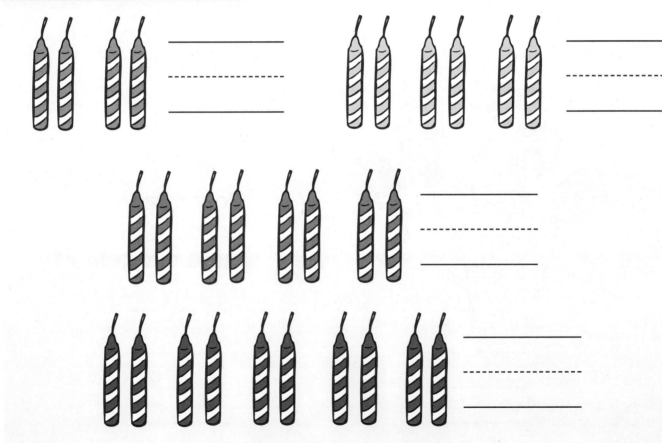

We learned how to make a Cloud Town special treat—ice cream cones! You can make them, too! **Draw scoops to match the number on each cone.**

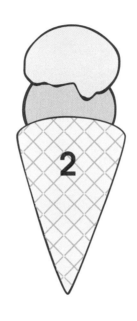

2

4

6

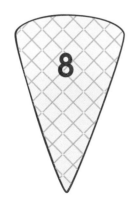

8

10

Excellent job! Put your carrot sticker in your basket and jump ahead.

Counting by Groups (83)

We are going to Guthry's house, but we need to meet up with Dash first. Can you help us get to her? **Color a path from 2 to 50 by skip-counting by twos.**

2

17

28

105

4

26

24

6

8

22

10

7

20

12

14

16

18

Terrific! Put your cupcake flag sticker on the Certificate of Completion. Then jump ahead for more adventures in counting.

Review **85**

I'm carrying so many presents for Guthry!
Look at the pictures below. Circle the one in each group that shows "more."

Breezy blew up all these balloons! Who has less? That's right, I do! Now look at each set of pictures below. **Color the balloons. Then circle the group that shows "less."**

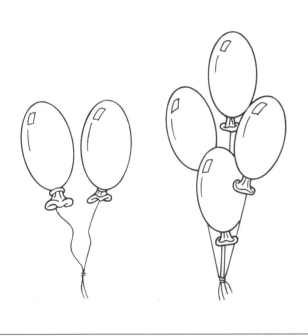

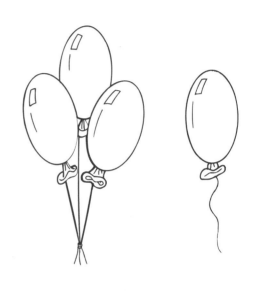

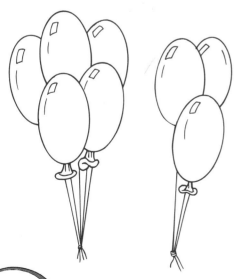

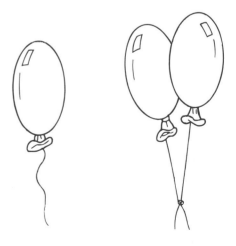

Stupendous! Put your carrot sticker in your basket and jump ahead to the next level!

More and Less   (87)

Farmer Hank and I are in the Party Hat Forest.
Circle the tree with the most hats. Then put an X on the tree with the least hats.

Cloud bowling is a fun Cloud Town sport.
Count the pins in each lane. Write the numbers in the spaces above the pins. Then answer the questions at the bottom by circling the words "more" or "less."

Dash

Bello

Farmer
Hank

Hopsalot

Did Dash knock down more or less than Farmer Hank?
Did Farmer Hank knock down more or less than Bello?

Kite-skiing in Cloud Town is also fun! **Look at the four pictures below. Circle the thing in each picture that shows "more."**

Look at all the birthday cards for Guthry! **Count the cards and write how many each mouse has. Circle the mouse with the most cards. Put an X on the mouse with the least.**

On a separate piece of paper, draw a birthday card for Guthry!

Stupendous! Put your carrot sticker in your basket and jump ahead to the next level!

More and Less **91**

Hopsalot's Hints

When you have many things to count, try **skip-counting by twos, fives,** or **tens** to make a big job go faster.

It is almost time for Guthry's party! Help me get everything ready. **Circle the group in each set that has "more."**

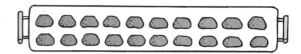

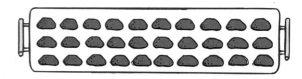

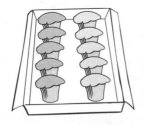

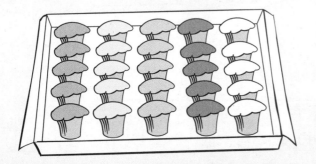

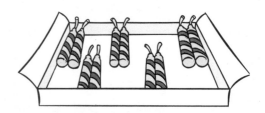

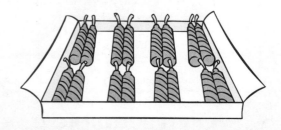

Jumping gerbils! The rainbow snowball maker is stuck on HIGH! Help us catch the falling snowballs.

Write how many snowballs there are under each cone.

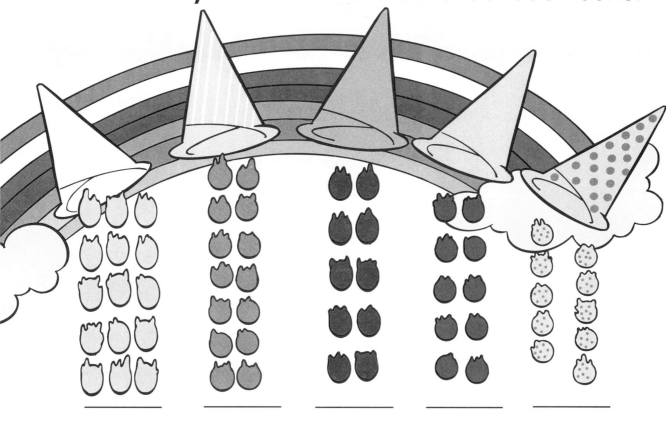

Circle the cone with the most snowballs.

At last! We are at Guthry the Giant's party! Help us surprise him for his birthday!

Happy Birthday,

To get through the maze, follow each number that is more than the one next to it.

Guthry!

FINISH

13
14
15
16
25
24
23
22
21
20
19
18
18
17
17
16
15
14
13
12
1
2
3

Stupendous! You did it! Put your party flag sticker on the Certificate of Completion.

Review 95

Answer Key

PAGE 66	trace: 1, 2, 3, 4, 5
PAGE 67	trace: 6, 7, 8, 9, 10
PAGE 68	connect-the-dots airplane
PAGE 69	write: 4, 10, 7, 15, 12; 13 cupcakes have pink frosting
PAGE 70	write: 3, 6, 9, 5; 23 buttons altogether
PAGE 71	circle 20 balloons
PAGE 72	write: 6, 4, 8, 9; 27 raisins altogether
PAGE 73	draw raisins; 7, 6, 3, 2; 18 raisins in all
PAGES 74–75	connect-the-dots Breezy, the cat
PAGE 76	10 of each color ribbon; 40 ribbons altogether
PAGE 77	10 of each color gumdrop; 40 gumdrops altogether
PAGE 78	2 steps
PAGE 79	10 kids are carrying each cupcake; 40 kids in all
PAGE 80	write: 5 under each color block; 25 altogether
PAGE 81	write: 5, 10, 5; 20 balloons altogether
PAGE 82	write: 2, 4, 6, 8, 10
PAGE 83	draw scoops: 4, 2, 6, 8, 10

PAGES 84–85	color: 2, 4, 6, 8, 10, 12, 14, 16, 18, 20, 22, 24, 26, 28, 30, 32, 34, 36, 38, 40, 42, 44, 46, 48, 50
PAGE 86	circle: 3 bows; 4 presents; 2 scoops; 6 cupcakes
PAGE 87	circle: 2 balloons; 1 balloon; 3 balloons; 1 balloon
PAGE 88	circle the tree with 7 hats; put an "X" on tree with 2 hats.
PAGE 89	write: 3, 4, 5, 6; Dash knocked down less than Farmer Hank; Farmer Hank knocked down more than Bello
PAGE 90	circle: kite with 9 bows; shirt with 9 buttons; cookie with 6 raisins; ice cream cone with 10 scoops
PAGE 91	write: 1, 2, 6, 4, 5, 3, 7; circle the mouse with 7 cards; put an "X" on the mouse with 1 card
PAGE 92	circle: 20 cups; 30 gumdrops; 25 cupcakes; 16 candles
PAGE 93	write: 15, 14, 10, 10, 10; circle: the cone with 15 snowballs
PAGES 94–95	trace a path: 1–25